STEP-BY-STEP

50 Low Calorie Desserts

STEP-BY-STEP

50 Low Calorie Desserts

Christine France

Photography by Don Last

LORENZ BOOKS

LONDON • NEW YORK • SYDNEY • BATH

First published in 1995 by Lorenz Books

© Anness Publishing Limited 1995

ˈLorenz Books is an imprint of
Anness Publishing Limited
1 Boundary Row
London SE1 8HP

ISBN 1 85967 095 4

A CIP catalogue record is available from the British Library.

Publisher: Joanna Lorenz
Editor: Joanne Rippin
Designer: Peter Laws
Jacket Designer: Peter Butler
Photographer: Don Last
Stylist: Fiona Tillett

The author wishes to thank the following manufacturers for the use of equipment:
Gas hob from Zanussi UK
Food processor from Philips Electrical UK
Saucepans from Prestige Group UK

MEASUREMENTS
Three sets of equivalent measurements have been provided in the recipes here, in
the following order: Metric, Imperial and American. It is essential that units of
measurement are not mixed within each recipe. Where conversions result in
awkward numbers, these have been rounded for convenience, but are accurate
enough to produce successful results.

Typeset by MC Typeset Ltd, Rochester, Kent
Printed and bound in Hong Kong

CONTENTS

INTRODUCTION

If you're trying to cut down on calories or fat in your diet, the chances are that the foods you most crave are the sweet ones – lovely, luscious desserts and proper puddings. And the reason you crave them is that you think that they're denied you on a sensible low-calorie diet.

The good news is that you really don't have to give up puddings – if you stick to the recipes in this book. They are all specially designed to fit into a healthy, lighter diet, all have fewer than 200 calories per portion, and are low in fat.

The secret of cutting calories and staying healthy is not to concentrate only on *counting* calories to the exclusion of other considerations – it's also important to make sure that your whole diet has a good nutritional balance. Recent health reports show that most of us need to cut down on fat, and desserts are one area in which it's easy to do just that.

Nowadays, we're lucky enough to have available lots of delicious, lighter alternatives to ingredients such as cream – so even classic, rich dishes can be lightened quite easily. You'll find that, after a while, your taste will change, and in many cases you will actually prefer the lighter, fresher flavours of low-fat desserts to some of the over-rich alternatives.

We all know we should be eating more fruit – it's recommended that we should eat five pieces or portions of fresh fruit or vegetables each day, so it's important to include plenty of fresh fruit in your desserts for fibre, essential vitamins and minerals. These recipes make full use of the wonderfully abundant choice of fruits we now have all year round.

So whether you're cutting calories to lose weight, or just trying to lighten your diet, this book will help you do it without giving up the sweet things in life!

Equipment

A basic selection of kitchen equipment is all you need for making successful desserts.

Balloon whisk
For hand-beating of sauces, whisking egg whites and incorporating air into other light mixtures.

Cannelle knife
For cutting decorative grooves in fruit, etc.

Chopping board
Non-porous chopping boards, such as those made from polypropylene, are preferable to wooden ones, which can absorb flavours and may harbour bacteria.

Citrus zester
Used for removing the coloured part of the rind from oranges, lemons or limes, without any of the white pith.

Corer
Used for removing cores from fruit such as apple or pears.

Electric whisk
For effortless whisking of egg whites, and beating and creaming mixtures.

Food processor
Makes smooth fruit purées and easy whipped desserts and saves lots of time and effort when chopping or slicing ingredients.

Graters
Essential for ingredients such as nutmeg, fruit or rind.

Heart-shaped or fluted tins
These make simple mousses, jellies or ices into sophisticated desserts.

Honey twirl
For spooning honey with no mess!

Ice cream scoop
For scooping sorbets and ices easily and decoratively.

Juice squeezer
Made from porcelain, glass or tough plastic, for squeezing the juice from citrus fruit.

Measuring jugs
Standard kitchen measuring jugs are useful for measuring liquid and dry ingredients accurately.

Measuring spoons and cups
Standard measuring spoons or cups are essential for measuring small quantities of ingredients accurately.

Melon baller
Useful for removing the flesh from fruit like melons in decorative spherical shapes.

Mixing bowls
A good selection of mixing bowls of various sizes is essential in any kitchen.

Pastry brush
Used for brushing oil, milk or beaten egg.

Peeler
A strong, swivel-blade peeler is the best choice for fruit.

Ramekins
Individual, heatproof dishes useful for desserts.

Rubber spatula
Useful for scraping out bowls and folding in ingredients.

Sharp knives
Essential for safe, efficient preparation of fruit, etc.

Sieve
For sifting powdered ingredients or fine sprinkling of icing sugar, etc. Also for sieving puréed fruit.

Slotted draining spoon
Use this for lifting and draining poached fruit.

Wooden spoons
For stirring and creaming ingredients.

electric whisk

ice cream scoop

honey twirl

wooden spoons

pastry brush

sieve

mixing bowls

food processor

graters

fluted tins

heart-shaped tins

opping board

cannelle knife

corer

peeler

melon baller

citrus zester

measuring spoons

measuring jug

slotted
draining spoon

sharp knives

balloon whisk

ramekin

rubber spatula

juice squeezer

Fruits

Thanks to imports from all over the world, we now have a huge variety of fresh fruits available all year round, and new ones are appearing all the time. Make use of their natural sweetness and colour in healthy desserts.

ORCHARD AND VINE FRUITS

Apples and pears
These are very versatile fruits; both dessert and culinary varieties can be cooked.

Grapes
The many varieties of grapes vary in colour from pale green to deep purple. The sweetness also varies, so taste before you buy. Seedless grapes are usually sweet.

CITRUS FRUITS

Grapefruit
These can have green, yellow or pink-flushed skin, with yellow, green or pink flesh. The pink-fleshed or ruby varieties are the sweetest.

Kumquats
Kumquats are tiny relatives of oranges and can be eaten whole, either raw or cooked.

Lemons and limes
These are interchangeable in most recipes, but lime has a more scented, intense flavour, so use it more sparingly.

Oranges
Ready to eat just as they are, or use the rind, juice and segments in desserts.

Satsumas
Satsumas, tangerines, mandarins and clementines are some of the varieties of small citrus fruits which are mostly interchangeable.

SOFT FRUITS

Blackberries
Blackberries can be found growing wild or are cultivated. Brambles are usually smaller than cultivated blackberries, with a stronger flavour. When they are not available, use raspberries or blackcurrants.

Blackcurrants
Blackcurrants, redcurrants and white currants are usually sold 'on the string', that is, on the stem. Keep a few on the stem for decoration.

Blueberries
Blueberries are best lightly poached, and are interchangeable with other berries.

Cranberries
Cranberries are too sharp to eat raw, but their intense flavour and stunning colour make them very good for cooking. Both frozen and fresh cranberries are available.

Gooseberries
Dessert types of gooseberry are sweet and ready to eat. Cooking varieties are smaller, firm, green and slightly sharp.

Raspberries
Raspberries, loganberries and tayberries are all delicious, juicy berries which are interchangeable in recipes.

Strawberries
Strawberries are best eaten fresh and ripe; they tend to lose texture and colour if frozen, however.

STONE FRUITS

Apricots
Use apricots raw or lightly poached.

Cherries
The most famous cherry variety is morello. Cherries should be firm and glossy of whatever type.

Nectarines
This fruit is a relative of the peach, with a smooth skin and firm texture.

Peaches
Choose white peaches for the sweetest flavour, and yellow for a more aromatic flavour and firm texture.

Plums
There are many dessert and cooking plum varieties, ranging in colour from pale gold to black. For cooking, you can use slightly under-ripe plums.

EXOTIC FRUIT

Cape Gooseberry
Small, fragrant, pleasantly tart orange berries wrapped in a paper 'cape'.

Dates
Fresh dates are sweet and juicy, more succulent than dried dates.

Figs
Green- or purple-skinned fruit, with sweet, pinkish-red flesh. Eat figs whole or peeled.

Kiwi fruit
Kiwi fruit are available all year round. Peel them thinly and slice the bright-green flesh.

Lychees
A small fruit with a hard pink skin and sweet, perfumed juicy flesh.

Mango
The skin of mango may be green, red or golden, but the ripe flesh should always be golden yellow, sweet and juicy.

Melons
When testing for ripeness the stalk-end should give slightly when pressed.

Papaya
This has a smooth, yellow-green skin and pinkish, succulent flesh when ripe.

Passion-fruit
The purplish-brown skin is wrinkled when ripe. Cut the fruit in half and scoop out the juicy seeds.

Pineapple
When ripe, a leaf will pull out easily from the top and the smell will be fragrant.

Star-fruit
When sliced, this makes pretty five-pointed stars. The fruit is ripe when the edges begin to go brown.

RHUBARB
Technically rhubarb is a vegetable. The pink, forced, early rhubarb is the sweetest, and needs no peeling. Always discard the leaves and root ends.

Dairy Produce

There's now a great choice of dairy produce suitable for desserts; many of the products are low in fat, and make good substitutes for full-fat ingredients such as cream.

Buttermilk
Cultured buttermilk is skimmed milk with an added bacterial culture, to give it a natural tangy flavour.

Cottage cheese
A fresh, low-fat cheese which is also now available in half-fat versions.

Crème fraîche
A thick, soured cream made from single cream. Half-fat (light) crème fraîche has a fat content of only about 15%.

Eggs
The yolks contain most of the fat and calories; however, many desserts can be made just with the whites.

Fromage frais
A fresh, soft cheese, usually available in two fat levels: very low-fat (0.4%) or creamy (7.9%). It makes a good accompaniment for many desserts.

Low-fat or skimmed milk soft cheese
Soft cheeses made with semi-skimmed or skimmed milk are good substitutes for cream cheese.

Reduced-fat/Low-fat spreads
Between 25 and 60% fat; lower-fat ones are not suitable for cooking: check the label.

Ricotta cheese
A very soft, mild, white Italian cheese of 11% fat; rather like cottage cheese, but with a smooth, creamy texture. Use as fresh as possible.

Semi-skimmed milk
Has about 1.5–1.8% fat, and reduced amounts of vitamins A and D.

Skimmed milk
Skimmed milk has had virtually all its fat removed, to leave no more than 0.3%. Most of the vitamins A and D are also removed.

Tofu
A high-protein, low-fat curd made from soya milk, which is available in firm 'original' or softer 'silken' varieties.

YOGURT
Yogurt is a very nutritious, easily digestible food that is a wonderful substitute for cream in a low-fat diet.

Bio-yogurts
Bio-yogurts contain bacterial cultures that are believed to aid digestion and dietary balance. They have a mild, smooth taste, which is less acidic than traditional yogurts.

Diet yogurts
These may have as little as 0.1% fat content and are lower in total calories than other yogurts.

Greek yogurts
These are made from whole milk and have a fat content of around 10%; they have a rich, creamy flavour and a smooth texture. There are now 'light' versions of Greek yogurt available, with a reduced fat content.

Long-life yogurt
This is re-pasteurised after packing, and then vacuum-sealed so it keeps for about 3 months.

Low-fat yogurts
These have about a 1% fat content, and are available in either stirred or set varieties.

Organic yogurt
This is made entirely with organic produce.

Whole-milk yogurts
These are made with whole milk, so have a creamier taste and about a 3% fat content.

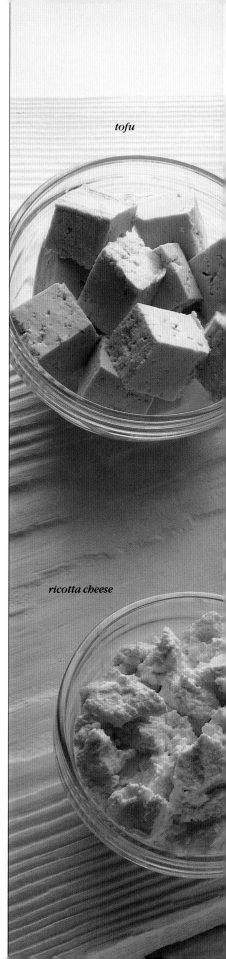

tofu

ricotta cheese

fromage frais

buttermilk

skimmed milk

skimmed-milk soft cheese

crème fraîche

yogurt

low-fat spread

cottage cheese

eggs

Storecupboard Ingredients

The following ingredients keep well and are good to have in the house for last minute or impulse desserts!

Artificial sweeteners
These can be liquid or granulated. They are a useful alternative to sugar for sweetening recipes whilst keeping down the calories. Most have about a tenth of the calories of sugar.

Dried fruit
An essential, nutritious storecupboard standby. Currants, sultanas, etc. are ready to use, but larger fruits should be soaked for several hours or simmered in water before use. Ready-to-eat dried apricots and prunes don't need any pre-soaking.

Fruit spreads and juices
Concentrated, unsweetened fruit spreads and juices can be kept handy as a good natural sweetener for all kinds of desserts.

Honey
Using this instead of sugar does not reduce the calories, but you can often use less honey than sugar, because honey tastes slightly sweeter and adds a pleasant flavour, especially if you choose a flower-scented honey.

Nuts
Almonds, walnuts, hazelnuts, etc add texture and flavour to desserts, but use them sparingly as they tend to be high in fat.

Plain or wholemeal flour
For healthy desserts, wholemeal flour is a good choice, but it is not always suitable and can sometimes give a heavy result. To avoid this, try using half wholemeal flour and half plain flour.

Porridge oats
High in soluble fibre, these are a healthy source of carbohydrate for all kinds of cooked puddings.

Powdered gelatine
Usually available in measured sachets, containing enough to set 600 ml/1 pint/2½ cups of liquid. Not suitable for vegetarians who should use agar agar instead.

Rose-water/Orange-flower water
Delicately perfumed flavourings for creamy dishes or fruit. Use sparingly, as they are very concentrated.

Skimmed-milk powder
A useful storecupboard standby for when you run out of fresh milk, or to add extra richness to skimmed-milk desserts.

Spices
Sweet spices such as cinnamon, mixed spice, cloves, allspice, star anise, cardamom and nutmeg are useful flavourings for many puddings and desserts.

Sugar
There is no calorific difference between white and brown sugars. Try to choose unrefined sugars, which contain no additives or colourings. The darker the sugar, the more flavour of molasses you will get. Useful choices for desserts are golden caster sugar, demerara sugar, and light and dark muscovado sugars. Icing sugar is also useful for light sprinkling over finished desserts.

Vanilla or almond essence
Try to choose natural essences or extracts if possible, for the best flavour.

Vanilla pods
Used whole for flavouring milk mixtures or custards. Can be rinsed and re-used several times.

fruit spread and juices

golden caster sugar

dark muscovado sugar

honey

nuts

skimmed-milk powder

vanilla
essence

vanilla pod

powdered gelatine

porridge oats

wholemeal flour

icing sugar

spices

plain flour

demerara sugar

light muscovado sugar

dried fruit

TECHNIQUES

It's worth mastering a few basic preparation skills to help you make successful, healthy desserts and puddings every time.

Peeling, Coring and Slicing Apples

Both cooking and eating apples are very simple to prepare, and very versatile.

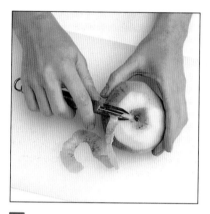

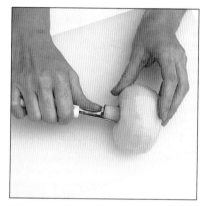

1 Use a peeler to peel the fruit as thinly as possible, in a spiral movement, turning the fruit as you go.

2 Use a corer to press through the centre of the apple and pull it out to remove the core (alternatively, cut the apple in quarters and cut out the core with a knife).

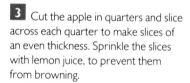

3 Cut the apple in quarters and slice across each quarter to make slices of an even thickness. Sprinkle the slices with lemon juice, to prevent them from browning.

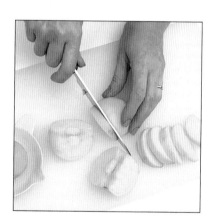

Peeling Peaches and Nectarines

The skin from these fruit can be tough if it is left on, so for certain recipes you need to peel them.

1 Immerse the whole fruit in a large pan of boiling water and boil for about 1 minute.

2 Lift the fruit out with a draining spoon and plunge the fruit into a bowl of cold water.

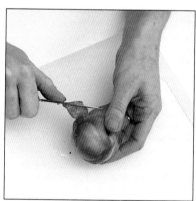

3 The skins should split slightly so you can peel them away from the fruit easily.

Grating Rind from Citrus Fruits

The outer, coloured rind of citrus fruit – sometimes called the zest – is full of flavour, but the white pith is very bitter, so methods for removing the rind without the pith are useful to know.

1 Choose unwaxed citrus fruit, or wash and dry the fruit thoroughly before use.

3 Alternatively, draw a citrus zester across the rind, removing fine strips of rind.

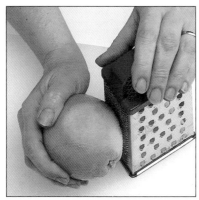

2 Use the fine gauge of a grater and rub the fruit against it to remove only the coloured rind and none of the bitter white pith beneath.

Segmenting Oranges

Many recipes need segments of orange to be removed without the membrane, which is very simple to do.

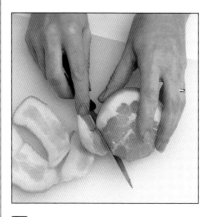

1 Peel the orange with a small, sharp knife, removing all the rind including the white pith.

2 Hold the orange over a bowl to catch the juice, and slice down either side of the separating membranes, to remove each segment cleanly.

3 Before discarding the membrane, hold it over the bowl and squeeze out any remaining juice.

Making Julienne Strips of Citrus Rind

A very simple decoration to sprinkle over desserts and puddings, hot or cold. Use oranges, lemons or limes.

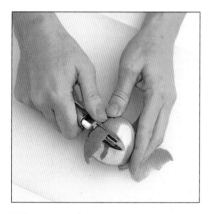

1 Using a vegetable peeler, pare a thin strip of the coloured rind from the fruit, avoiding the white pith underneath.

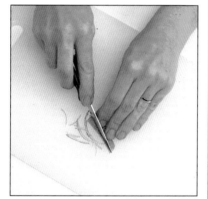

2 Stack the pieces of rind and use a sharp knife to cut into very thin shreds. Use the shreds straight away, or blanch them in boiling water for a few seconds, and then cool them in cold water. Dry them thoroughly on absorbent paper.

Stringing Redcurrants or Blackcurrants

These pretty berry fruits are usually sold 'on the string'; here is a simple way to remove them.

1 Hold the fruit by the stalk in one hand over a bowl and pull the prongs of a fork through, to pull the currants off.

2 If the currants have been frozen on the stem, they can be removed by simply shaking them in a polythene box, to break off the stalks.

Preparing Mango

Mango has a beautiful golden, sweet and juicy flesh which is delicious just as it is, or in all kinds of desserts.

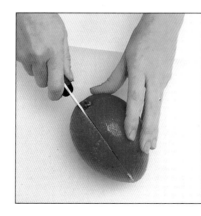

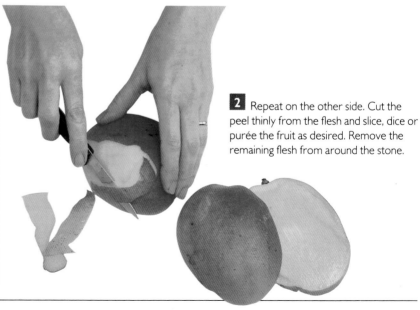

1 To find out which way the stone lies, lay the fruit on a flat surface. The stone will be parallel to the surface. Cut horizontally through the fruit, keeping the knife blade in line with, and close to, the stone.

2 Repeat on the other side. Cut the peel thinly from the flesh and slice, dice or purée the fruit as desired. Remove the remaining flesh from around the stone.

Cooked Fruit Purée

Fruit purées are a useful base for many desserts, and also make very good, fat-free sauces.

1 Cook the fruit in a pan, with a small amount of water or sugar, until soft. If you use sugar alone, heat the fruit very gently until the fruit juice begins to run and the sugar dissolves.

2 Remove any stones from the fruit and then tip it into a food processor or blender and process until smooth. The mixture may then need to be sieved.

Separating Eggs

There are many ways to separate eggs, but this one is by far the easiest.

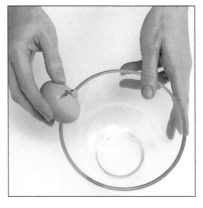

1 Tap the egg sharply against the edge of a mixing bowl, or tap it with the back of a knife, to break the shell across the middle.

2 Holding the egg over the bowl, carefully pull the two halves of shell apart and gently tip the yolk from one half to the other, allowing the white to run into the bowl.

Sieving Fruit

Many recipes call for fruit to be sieved, to remove pips or skin. Firmer fruit, such as apple, should be cooked before you sieve them; soft fruit, like raspberries, can be sieved raw, and spooned straight on to the plate.

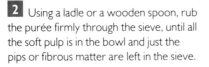

1 If the fruit is firm, purée it first in a blender or food processor. Tip it into a sieve over a large bowl.

2 Using a ladle or a wooden spoon, rub the purée firmly through the sieve, until all the soft pulp is in the bowl and just the pips or fibrous matter are left in the sieve.

Whisking Egg Whites

Egg whites can increase in volume by about eight times, making mixtures light and airy.

1 Place the egg whites in a completely clean, grease-free mixing bowl. If any grease or even a speck of egg yolk is present, the egg whites will not hold air bubbles. Use one half of shell to remove any specks of yolk.

2 Use a balloon whisk in a wide bowl for the greatest volume, but an electric hand whisk will also do an efficient job. A copper bowl will give a greater bulk, but this is not essential.

3 Whisk the whites until they are firm enough to hold either soft or stiff peaks when you lift the whisk, according to what's needed in the recipe. Use immediately.

Dissolving Gelatine

It's important to dissolve gelatine correctly, or it can spoil the texture and set of your finished dessert.

1 Place 45 ml/3 tbsp of very hot water per sachet of gelatine in a small bowl.

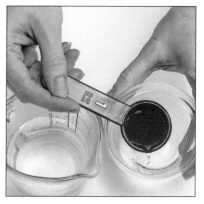

2 Sprinkle the gelatine over the liquid. Always add gelatine to the liquid, never the other way round.

3 Stir briskly until the gelatine is completely dissolved. There should be no visible crystals and the liquid should be clear. If necessary, stand the container in a pan of hot water over a low heat until dissolved. Do not allow gelatine to boil.

Unmoulding Gelatine-set Mixtures

Moulded gelatine desserts always look impressive and are really very easy to make. The dessert must be thoroughly chilled before you start to turn it out.

1 Have ready a serving plate that has been rinsed with cold water. Run the tip of a knife around the edge of the moulded mixture, to loosen it from the mould.

2 Dip the mould briefly into a bowl of hot water. One or two seconds is usually enough: longer could melt the mixture too much.

3 Quickly place the plate on top of the mould and turn them over together. Holding the plate and mould together, shake firmly to dislodge the dessert; then remove the mould. If it does not lift off easily, repeat the shaking until it does.

Lining a Swiss-roll Tin

Lining cake tins is always helpful to prevent mixtures from sticking, especially if they're low in fat. Use non-stick baking paper rather than greaseproof paper for easy removal.

1 Cut a piece of non-stick baking paper large enough to line the base and sides of the tin.

2 Place the tin in the centre of the paper, and then make a cut from each corner of the paper to the corner of the tin.

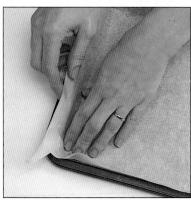

3 Place the paper in the tin and smooth into the sides, overlapping the paper corners so they fit neatly.

Cherry Pancakes

These pancakes are virtually fat-free, and lower in calories and higher in fibre than traditional ones. Serve with a spoonful of natural yogurt or fromage frais.

Serves 4

Calories per portion about 185

INGREDIENTS
FOR THE PANCAKES
50 g/2 oz/½ cup plain flour
50 g/2 oz/⅓ cup plain wholemeal flour
pinch of salt
1 egg white
150 ml/¼ pint/⅔ cup skimmed milk
150 ml/¼ pint/⅔ cup water
a little oil for frying

FOR THE FILLING
425 g/15 oz can black cherries in juice
7.5 ml/1½ tsp arrowroot

skimmed milk

wholemeal flour

plain flour

black cherries

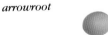
arrowroot

egg

1 Sift the flours and salt into a bowl, adding any bran left in the sieve to the bowl at the end.

2 Make a well in the centre of the flour and add the egg white. Gradually beat in the milk and water, whisking hard until all the liquid is incorporated and the batter is smooth and bubbly.

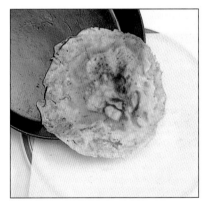

3 Heat a non-stick pan with a small amount of oil until the pan is very hot. Pour in just enough batter to cover the base of the pan, swirling the pan to cover the base evenly.

4 Cook until the pancake is set and golden, and then turn to cook the other side. Remove to a sheet of absorbent paper and then cook the remaining batter, to make about eight pancakes.

5 Drain the cherries, reserving the juice. Blend about 30 ml/2 tbsp of the juice from the can of cherries with the arrowroot in a saucepan. Stir in the rest of the juice. Heat gently, stirring, until boiling. Stir over a moderate heat for about 2 minutes, until thickened and clear.

COOK'S TIP

If fresh cherries are in season, cook them gently in enough apple juice just to cover them, and then thicken the juice with arrowroot as in Step 5.

The basic pancakes will freeze very successfully. Interleave them with non-stick or absorbent paper, overwrap them in polythene and seal. Freeze for up to six months. Thaw at room temperature.

6 Add the cherries and stir until thoroughly heated. Spoon the cherries into the pancakes and fold them in quarters.

Golden Ginger Compote

Warm, spicy and full of sun-ripened ingredients – this is the perfect winter dessert.

Serves 4

Calories per portion about 190

INGREDIENTS
200 g/7 oz/2 cups kumquats
200 g/7 oz/1¼ cups dried apricots
30 ml/2 tbsp sultanas
400 ml/14 fl oz/1⅔ cups water
1 orange
2.5 cm/1 in piece fresh root ginger
4 cardamom pods
4 cloves
30 ml/2 tbsp clear honey
15 ml/1 tbsp flaked almonds, toasted

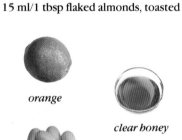

orange

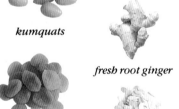

clear honey

kumquats

fresh root ginger

dried apricots

flaked almonds

cloves

cardamom pods

sultanas

1 Wash the kumquats, and, if they are large, cut them in half. Place them in a pan with the apricots, sultanas and water. Bring to the boil.

2 Pare the rind thinly from the orange and add to the pan. Peel and grate the ginger and add to the pan. Lightly crush the cardamom pods and add them to the pan, with the cloves.

COOK'S TIP

Use ready-to-eat dried apricots. Reduce the liquid to 300 ml/½ pint/ 1¼ cups, add the apricots for the last 5 minutes of cooking.

3 Reduce the heat, cover the pan and leave to simmer gently for about 30 minutes, or until the fruit is tender, stirring occasionally.

4 Squeeze the juice from the orange and add to the pan with honey to sweeten to taste, sprinkle with flaked almonds and serve warm.

Strawberry and Apple Crumble

A high-fibre, healthier version of the classic apple crumble. Raspberries can be used instead of strawberries, either fresh or frozen. Serve warm, with skimmed-milk custard or yogurt.

Serves 4

Calories per portion about 155

INGREDIENTS
450 g/1 lb cooking apples
150 g/5 oz/1¼ cups strawberries, hulled
30 ml/2 tbsp granulated sweetener
2.5 ml/½ tsp ground cinnamon
30 ml/2 tbsp orange juice

FOR THE CRUMBLE
45 ml/3 tbsp plain wholemeal flour
50 g/2 oz/⅔ cup porridge oats
25 g/1 oz/⅛ cup low-fat spread

porridge oats   *granulated sweetener*

low-fat spread

wholemeal flour

strawberries

cooking apples

ground cinnamon

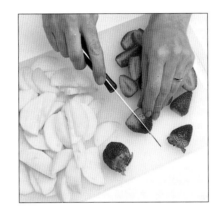

1 Preheat the oven to 180°C/350°F/ Gas 4. Peel, core and slice the apples. Halve the strawberries.

2 Toss together the apples, strawberries, sweetener, cinnamon and orange juice. Tip into a 1.2-litre/ 2-pint/5-cup ovenproof dish, or four individual dishes.

3 Combine the flour and oats in a bowl and mix in the low-fat spread with a fork.

4 Sprinkle the crumble evenly over the fruit. Bake for 40–45 minutes (20–25 minutes for individual dishes), until golden brown and bubbling. Serve warm, with custard or yogurt.

Floating Islands in Hot Plum Sauce

An unusual, low-fat pudding that is simpler to make than it looks. The plum sauce can be made in advance, and reheated just before you cook the meringues.

Serves 4

Calories per portion about 90

INGREDIENTS
450 g/1 lb red plums
300 ml/½ pint/1¼ cups apple juice
2 egg whites
30 ml/2 tbsp concentrated apple-juice syrup
freshly grated nutmeg

apple juice

red plums

eggs

concentrated apple-juice syrup

nutmeg

COOK'S TIP

A bottle of concentrated apple juice is a useful storecupboard sweetener, but if you don't have any, use a little honey instead.

1 Halve the plums and remove the stones. Place them in a wide pan, with the apple juice.

2 Bring to the boil and then cover with a lid and leave to simmer gently until the plums are tender.

3 Meanwhile, place the egg whites in a clean, dry bowl and whisk them until they hold soft peaks.

4 Gradually whisk in the apple juice syrup, whisking until the meringue holds fairly firm peaks.

5 Using a tablespoon, scoop the meringue mixture into the gently simmering plum sauce. You may need to cook the 'islands' in two batches.

6 Cover and allow to simmer gently for 2–3 minutes, until the meringues are just set. Serve straight away, sprinkled with a little freshly grated nutmeg.

Chunky Apple Bake

This filling, economical family pudding is a good way to use up slightly stale bread – any type of bread will do, but wholemeal is richest in fibre.

Serves 4

Calories per portion about 180

INGREDIENTS
450 g/1 lb Bramley or other cooking apples
75 g/3 oz wholemeal bread, without crusts
115 g/4 oz/½ cup cottage cheese
45 ml/3 tbsp light muscovado sugar
200 ml/7 fl oz/⅞ cup semi-skimmed milk
5 ml/1 tsp demerara sugar

cottage cheese

semi-skimmed milk

demerara sugar

cooking apples

wholemeal bread   *light muscovado sugar*

1 Preheat the oven to 220°C/425°F/ Gas Mark 7. Peel the apples, cut them in quarters and remove the cores.

2 Roughly chop the apples into even-size pieces, about 1 cm/½ in across.

3 Cut the bread into 1 cm/½ in dice.

4 Toss together the apples, bread, cottage cheese and muscovado sugar.

5 Stir in the milk and then tip the mixture into a wide ovenproof dish. Sprinkle with the demerara sugar.

6 Bake for 30–35 minutes, or until golden brown and bubbling. Serve hot.

COOK'S TIP
You may need to adjust the amount of milk used, depending on the dryness of the bread; the more stale the bread, the more milk it will absorb.

Baked Apples in Honey and Lemon

A classic mix of flavours in a healthy, traditional family pudding. Serve warm, with skimmed-milk custard.

Serves 4

Calories per portion about 105

INGREDIENTS
4 medium-size cooking apples
15 ml/1 tbsp clear honey
grated rind and juice of 1 lemon
15 ml/1 tbsp low-fat spread

clear honey

cooking apples

lemon

low-fat spread

COOK'S TIP

This recipe can also be cooked in the microwave to save time. Place the apples in a microwave-safe dish and cover them with a lid or pierced clear film. Microwave on FULL POWER (100%) for 9–10 minutes.

1 Preheat the oven to 180°C/350°F/ Gas 4. Remove the cores from the apples, leaving them whole.

2 With a cannelle or sharp knife, cut lines through the apple skin at intervals and place in an ovenproof dish.

3 Mix together the honey, lemon rind, juice and low-fat spread.

4 Spoon the mixture into the apples and cover the dish with foil or a lid. Bake for 40–45 minutes, or until the apples are tender. Serve with skimmed-milk custard.

Filo Chiffon Pie

Filo pastry is low in fat and is very easy to use. Keep a pack in the freezer, ready to make impressive puddings like this one.

Serves 3

Calories per portion about 180

INGREDIENTS
500 g/1¼ lb pink rhubarb
5 ml/1 tsp mixed spice
finely grated rind and juice
    of 1 orange
15 ml/1 tbsp granulated sweetener
15 g/½ oz/1 tbsp butter
3 sheets filo pastry

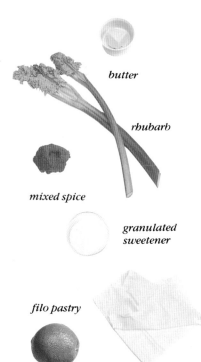

butter

rhubarb

mixed spice

granulated sweetener

filo pastry

orange

VARIATION

Other fruit such as apples, pears or peaches can be used in this pie – try it with whatever is in season.

1 Preheat the oven to 200°C/400°F/ Gas 6. Trim the leaves and ends from the rhubarb sticks and chop them in 2.5 cm/ 1 in pieces. Place them in a bowl.

2 Add the mixed spice, orange rind and juice and sweetener and toss well to coat evenly. Tip the rhubarb into a 1-litre/ 1¾-pint/4-cup pie dish.

3 Melt the butter and brush it over the pastry. Lift the pastry on to the pie dish, butter-side up, and crumple it up to form a chiffon effect, covering the pie completely.

4 Place the dish on a baking sheet and bake it for 20 minutes, until golden brown. Reduce the heat to 180°C/350°F/ Gas 4 and bake for a further 10–15 minutes, until the rhubarb is tender. Serve warm.

Coconut Dumplings with Apricot Sauce

These delicate little dumplings are very simple to make and cook in minutes. The sharp flavour of the sauce offsets the creamy dumplings beautifully.

Serves 4

Calories per portion about 120

INGREDIENTS
FOR THE DUMPLINGS
75 g/3 oz/⅓ cup cottage cheese
1 egg white
30 ml/2 tbsp low-fat spread
15 ml/1 tbsp light muscovado sugar
30 ml/2 tbsp self-raising wholemeal
   flour
finely grated rind of ½ lemon
30 ml/2 tbsp desiccated coconut,
   toasted

FOR THE SAUCE
225 g/8 oz can apricot halves in
   natural juice
15 ml/1 tbsp lemon juice

1 Half-fill a steamer with boiling water and put it on to boil. Alternatively, place a heatproof plate over a pan of boiling water.

2 Beat together the cottage cheese, egg white and low-fat spread until they are evenly mixed.

3 Stir in the sugar, flour, lemon rind and coconut, mixing everything evenly to a fairly firm dough.

4 Place 8–12 spoonfuls of the mixture in the steamer or on the plate, leaving a space between them.

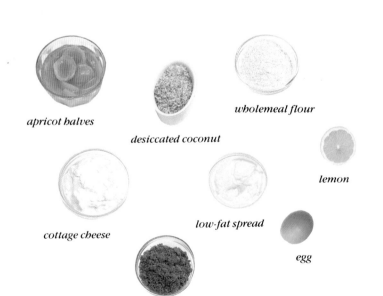

apricot halves

desiccated coconut

wholemeal flour

lemon

cottage cheese

low-fat spread

egg

light muscovado sugar

COOK'S TIP

The mixture should be quite stiff: if it's not stiff enough to hold its shape, stir in a little more flour.

5 Cover the steamer or pan tightly with a lid or a plate and steam for about 10 minutes, until the dumplings have risen and are firm to the touch.

6 Meanwhile, purée the can of apricots and stir in the lemon juice. Pour into a small pan and heat until boiling, then serve with the dumplings. Sprinkle with extra coconut to serve.

Cornflake-topped Peach Bake

A golden, crisp-crusted, family pudding that's made in minutes, from storecupboard ingredients.

Serves 4

Calories per portion about 180

INGREDIENTS
415 g/14½ oz can peach slices in juice
30 ml/2 tbsp sultanas
1 cinnamon stick
strip of fresh orange rind
30 ml/2 tbsp butter or margarine
50 g/2 oz/1½ cups cornflakes
15 ml/1 tbsp sesame seeds

cinnamon stick

sesame seeds   *sultanas*

peach slices

butter   *orange rind*

cornflakes

COOK'S TIP
If you don't have a cinnamon stick, sprinkle in about 2.5 ml/½ tsp ground cinnamon instead.

1 Preheat the oven to 200°C/400°F/ Gas 6. Drain the peaches, reserving the juice, and arrange the peach slices in a shallow ovenproof dish.

2 Place the peach juice, sultanas, cinnamon stick and orange rind in a pan and bring to the boil. Simmer, uncovered, for 3–4 minutes, to reduce the liquid by about half. Remove the cinnamon stick and orange rind and spoon the syrup over the peaches.

3 Melt the butter or margarine in a small pan and stir in the cornflakes and sesame seeds.

4 Spread the cornflake mixture over the fruit. Bake for 15–20 minutes, or until the topping is crisp and golden. Serve hot.

Sultana and Couscous Puddings

Most couscous on the market now is the pre-cooked variety, which needs only the minimum of cooking, but check the pack instructions first to make sure. Serve hot, with yogurt or skimmed-milk custard.

Serves 4

Calories per portion about 170

INGREDIENTS
50 g/2 oz/⅓ cup sultanas
475 ml/16 fl oz/2 cups apple juice
90 g/3½ oz/1 cup couscous
2.5 ml/½ tsp mixed spice

apple juice

couscous

mixed spice

sultanas

COOK'S TIP

If you prefer, these puddings can be cooked in the microwave oven instead of steaming. Use individual microwave-safe basins or teacups, cover them and microwave on **FULL POWER** (100%) for 8–10 minutes.

1 Lightly grease four 250 ml/8 fl oz/ 1-cup pudding basins or one 1-litre/ 1¾-pint/4-cup pudding basin. Place the sultanas and apple juice in a pan.

2 Bring the apple juice to the boil, and then cover the pan and leave to simmer gently for 2–3 minutes, to plump up the fruit. Using a slotted spoon, lift out about half the fruit and place it in the bottom of the basins.

3 Add the couscous and mixed spice to the pan and bring back to the boil, stirring. Cover and leave over a low heat for 8–10 minutes, or until the liquid is absorbed.

4 Spoon the couscous into the basins, spread it level, and then cover the basins tightly with foil. Place the basins in a steamer over boiling water, cover and steam for about 30 minutes. Run a knife around the edges, turn the puddings out carefully and serve straight away.

Baked Blackberry Cheesecake

This light, low-fat cheesecake is best made with wild blackberries, if they're available, but cultivated ones will do; or substitute other soft fruit, such as loganberries, raspberries or blueberries.

Serves 5

Calories per portion about 105

INGREDIENTS
175 g/6 oz/¾ cup cottage cheese
150 g/5 oz/⅔ cup low-fat natural
    yogurt
15 ml/1 tbsp plain wholemeal flour
25 g/1 oz/2 tbsp golden caster sugar
1 egg
1 egg white
finely grated rind and juice of
    ½ lemon
200 g/7 oz/2 cups fresh or frozen and
    thawed blackberries

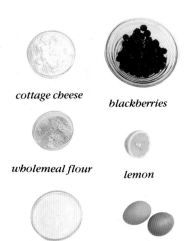

cottage cheese   *blackberries*

wholemeal flour   *lemon*

natural yogurt   *eggs*

golden caster sugar

COOK'S TIP

If you prefer to use canned blackberries, choose those canned in natural juice and drain the fruit well before adding it to the cheesecake mixture. The juice can be served with the cheesecake, but this will increase the total calories.

1 Preheat the oven to 180°C/350°F/ Gas 4. Lightly grease and base-line an 18 cm/7 in sandwich tin.

2 Place the cottage cheese in a food processor and process until smooth. Alternatively, rub it through a sieve, to obtain a smooth mixture.

3 Add the yogurt, flour, sugar, egg and egg white and mix. Add the lemon rind, juice and blackberries, reserving a few for decoration.

4 Tip the mixture into the prepared tin and bake it for 30–35 minutes, or until it's just set. Turn off the oven and leave for a further 30 minutes.

5 Run a knife around the edge of the cheesecake, and then turn it out. Remove the lining paper and place the cheesecake on a warm serving plate.

6 Decorate the cheesecake with the reserved blackberries and serve it warm.

Chocolate, Date and Walnut Pudding

Proper puddings are not totally taboo when you're cutting calories or fat – this one stays within the rules! Serve hot, with yogurt or skimmed-milk custard.

Serves 4

Calories per portion about 165

INGREDIENTS
25 g/1 oz/4 tbsp chopped walnuts
25 g/1 oz/2 tbsp chopped dates
2 eggs
5 ml/1 tsp vanilla essence
30 ml/2 tbsp golden caster sugar
45 ml/3 tbsp plain wholemeal flour
15 ml/1 tbsp cocoa powder
30 ml/2 tbsp skimmed milk

vanilla essence

skimmed milk

wholemeal flour

golden caster sugar

eggs

cocoa powder

walnuts

dates

1 Preheat the oven to 180°C/350°F/Gas 4. Grease a 1.2-litre/2-pint/5-cup pudding basin and place a small circle of greaseproof or non-stick baking paper in the base. Spoon in the walnuts and dates.

2 Separate the eggs and place the yolks in a bowl, with the vanilla and sugar. Place the bowl over a pan of hot water and whisk until the mixture is thick and pale.

3 Sift the flour and cocoa into the mixture and fold them in with a metal spoon. Stir in the milk, to soften the mixture slightly. Whisk the egg whites until they hold soft peaks and fold them in.

4 Spoon the mixture into the basin and bake for 40–45 minutes, or until the pudding is well risen and firm to the touch. Run a knife around the pudding to loosen it from the basin, and then turn it out and serve straight away.

Grilled Nectarines with Ricotta and Spice

This easy dessert is good at any time of year – use canned peach halves if fresh ones are not available.

Serves 4

Calories per portion about 150

INGREDIENTS
4 ripe nectarines or peaches
15 ml/1 tbsp light muscovado sugar
115 g/4 oz/½ cup ricotta cheese or
    fromage frais
2.5 ml/½ tsp ground star anise

nectarines

light muscovado sugar

ricotta cheese

ground star anise

1 Cut the nectarines in half and remove the stones.

2 Arrange the nectarines, cut-side upwards, in a wide flameproof dish or on a baking sheet.

3 Stir the sugar into the ricotta or fromage frais. Using a teaspoon, spoon the mixture into the hollow of each nectarine half.

4 Sprinkle with the star anise. Place under a moderately hot grill for 6–8 minutes, or until the nectarines are hot and bubbling. Serve warm.

COOK'S TIP
Star anise has a warm, rich flavour – if you can't get it, try ground cloves or ground mixed spice instead.

Souffléed Rice Pudding

The fluffy egg whites in this unusually light rice pudding make the portions seem much more substantial, without adding lots of extra calories or fat.

Serves 4

Calories per portion about 200

INGREDIENTS
65 g/2½ oz/¼ cup short-grain rice
45 ml/3 tbsp clear honey
750 ml/1¼ pints/3⅔ cups semi-skimmed milk
1 vanilla pod or 2.5 ml/½ tsp vanilla essence
2 egg whites
5 ml/1 tsp freshly grated nutmeg

semi-skimmed milk

clear honey

short-grain rice

eggs

vanilla pod　*nutmeg*

COOK'S TIP

If you wish, use skimmed milk instead of semi-skimmed, but take care when it's simmering, as with so little fat, it tends to boil over very easily.

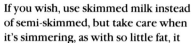

1 Place the rice, honey and milk in a heavy or non-stick pan and bring the milk to the boil. Add the vanilla pod, if using it.

2 Reduce the heat and put the lid on the pan. Leave to simmer gently for about 1–1¼ hours, stirring occasionally to prevent sticking, until most of the liquid has been absorbed.

3 Remove the vanilla pod, or if using vanilla essence, add this to the rice mixture now. Preheat the oven to 220°C/425°F/Gas 7.

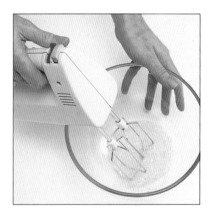

4 Place the egg whites in a clean, dry bowl and whisk them until they hold soft peaks.

5 Using a metal spoon or spatula, fold the egg whites evenly into the rice mixture and tip into a 1-litre/1¾-pint/4-cup ovenproof dish.

6 Sprinkle with grated nutmeg and bake for 15–20 minutes, until the pudding is well-risen and golden brown. Serve hot.

Grapes in Grape-yogurt Jelly

This light, refreshing dessert is fit for any special occasion and looks spectacular, but takes very little time to make.

Serves 4

Calories per portion about 105

INGREDIENTS
200 g/7 oz/1½ cups white seedless grapes
450 ml/¾ pint/1⅞ cups white grape juice
15 ml/1 tbsp/1 sachet powdered gelatine
125 g/4 oz/½ cup natural low-fat yogurt

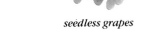

white grape juice

natural yogurt   *powdered gelatine*

seedless grapes

1 Reserve four sprigs of grapes for decoration and then cut the rest in half.

2 Divide the grapes between four stemmed glasses and tilt the glasses on one side, propping them firmly in a bowl of ice.

3 Place the grape juice in a pan and heat it until it's almost boiling. Remove it from the heat and sprinkle the gelatine over it, stirring to dissolve the gelatine.

4 Pour half the grape juice over the grapes and allow to set.

5 Cool the remaining grape juice but do not allow to set, then stir in the yogurt.

6 Stand the set glasses upright and pour in the yogurt mixture. Chill to set, then top each with a sprig of grapes before serving.

COOK'S TIP
For an easier version, stand the glasses upright rather than at an angle – then they can be set in the refrigerator rather than packed with ice.

Fresh Citrus Jelly

Fresh fruit jellies really are worth the effort – they're packed with fresh flavour, natural colour and vitamins – and they make a lovely fat-free dessert.

Serves 4

Calories per portion about 140

INGREDIENTS
3 medium-size oranges
1 lemon
1 lime
300 ml/½ pint/1¼ cups water
75 g/3 oz/⅓ cup golden caster sugar
15 ml/1 tbsp/1 sachet powdered
  gelatine
extra slices of fruit, to decorate

powdered gelatine

golden caster sugar

lime

oranges

lemon

1 With a sharp knife, cut all the peel and white pith from one orange and carefully remove the segments. Arrange the segments in the base of a 900 ml/1½-pint/3¾-cup mould or dish.

2 Remove some shreds of citrus rind with a zester and reserve them for decoration. Grate the remaining rind from the lemon and lime and one orange. Place all the grated rind in a pan, with the water and sugar.

3 Heat gently until the sugar has dissolved, without boiling. Remove from the heat. Squeeze the juice from all the rest of the fruit and stir it into the pan.

4 Strain the liquid into a measuring jug to remove the rind (you should have about 550 ml/1 pint/2½ cups: if necessary, make up the amount with water). Sprinkle the gelatine over the liquid and stir until it has completely dissolved.

5 Pour a little of the jelly over the orange segments and chill until set. Leave the remaining jelly at room temperature to cool, but do not allow it to set.

COOK'S TIP

To speed up the setting of the fruit segments in jelly, stand the dish in a bowl of ice. Or, if you're short of time, simply stir the segments into the liquid jelly, pour into a serving dish and set it all together.

6 Pour the remaining cooled jelly into the dish and chill until set. To serve, turn out the jelly and decorate it with the reserved citrus rind shreds and slices of citrus fruit.

Tofu Berry 'Cheesecake'

This summery 'cheesecake' is a very light and refreshing finish to any meal. Strictly speaking, it's not a cheesecake at all, as it's based on tofu – but who would guess?

Serves 6

Calories per portion about 190

INGREDIENTS
FOR THE BASE
50 g/2 oz/4 tbsp low-fat spread
30 ml/2 tbsp apple juice
115 g/4 oz/2½ cups bran flakes or
   other high-fibre cereal

FOR THE FILLING
285 g/10 oz/1½ cups tofu or
   skimmed-milk soft cheese
200 g/7 oz/⅞ cup low-fat natural
   yogurt
15 ml/1 tbsp/1 sachet powdered
   gelatine
60 ml/4 tbsp apple juice

FOR THE TOPPING
175 g/6 oz/1¾ cups mixed summer
   soft fruit, e.g. strawberries,
   raspberries, redcurrants,
   blackberries, etc (or frozen 'fruits of
   the forest')
30 ml/2 tbsp redcurrant jelly
30 ml/2 tbsp hot water

apple juice

bran flakes

summer fruit

tofu

natural yogurt

low-fat spread

COOK'S TIP
The lowest-calorie breakfast cereals are usually those which are highest in fibre, so it's worth checking the labels for comparisons.

1 For the base, place the low-fat spread and apple juice in a pan and heat them gently until the spread has melted. Crush the cereal and stir it into the pan.

2 Tip into a 23 cm/9 in round flan tin and press down firmly. Leave to set.

3 For the filling, place the tofu or cheese and yogurt in a food processor and process them until smooth. Dissolve the gelatine in the apple juice and stir the juice quickly into the tofu mixture.

4 Spread the tofu mixture over the chilled base, smoothing it evenly. Chill until the filling has set.

5 Remove the flan tin and place the 'cheesecake' on a serving plate.

6 Arrange the fruits over the top. Melt the redcurrant jelly with the hot water. Let it cool, and then spoon over the fruit to serve.

Watermelon, Ginger and Grapefruit Salad

This pretty, pink combination is very light and refreshing for any summer meal.

Serves 4

Calories per portion about 80

INGREDIENTS
500 g/1 lb/2 cups diced watermelon
  flesh
2 ruby or pink grapefruit
2 pieces stem ginger in syrup
30 ml/2 tbsp stem ginger syrup

watermelon flesh

ruby grapefruit

stem ginger in syrup

COOK'S TIP

Toss the fruits gently – grapefruit segments will break up easily and the appearance of the dish will be spoiled.

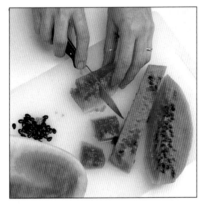

1 Remove any seeds from the watermelon and cut into bite-sized chunks.

2 Using a small sharp knife, cut away all the peel and white pith from the grapefruits and carefully lift out the segments, catching any juice in a bowl.

3 Finely chop the stem ginger and place in a serving bowl with the melon cubes and grapefruit segments, adding the reserved juice.

4 Spoon over the ginger syrup and toss the fruits lightly to mix evenly. Chill before serving.

Chocolate Vanilla Timbales

You really can allow yourself the occasional chocolate treat, especially if it's a dessert as light as this one.

Serves 6

Calories per portion about 100

INGREDIENTS
FOR THE TIMBALES
350 ml/12 fl oz/1½ cups semi-
   skimmed milk
30 ml/2 tbsp cocoa powder
2 eggs
5 ml/1 tsp vanilla essence
45 ml/3 tbsp granulated sweetener
15 ml/1 tbsp/1 sachet powdered
   gelatine
45 ml/3 tbsp hot water

FOR THE SAUCE
115 g/4 oz/½ cup light Greek yogurt
2.5 ml/½ tsp vanilla essence
extra cocoa powder, to sprinkle

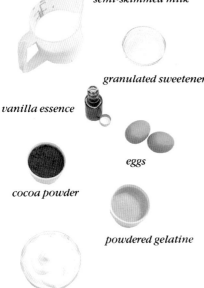

semi-skimmed milk

granulated sweetener

vanilla essence

eggs

cocoa powder

powdered gelatine

Greek yogurt

1 Place the milk and cocoa in a saucepan and stir until the milk is boiling. Separate the eggs and beat the egg yolks with the vanilla and sweetener in a bowl, until the mixture is pale and smooth. Gradually pour in the chocolate milk, beating well.

2 Return the mixture to the pan and stir constantly over a gentle heat, without boiling, until it's slightly thickened and smooth. Dissolve the gelatine in the hot water and then quickly stir it into the milk mixture. Let it cool until it's on the point of setting.

3 Whisk the egg whites until they hold soft peaks. Fold the egg whites quickly into the milk mixture. Spoon the timbale mixture into six individual moulds and chill them until set.

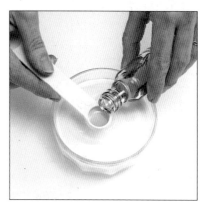

4 To serve, run a knife around the edge, dip the moulds quickly into hot water and turn out the chocolate timbales on to serving plates. For the sauce, stir together the yogurt and vanilla, spoon on to the plates and sprinkle with a little more cocoa powder.

Cappuccino Coffee Cups

Coffee-lovers will love this one – and it tastes rich and creamy, even though it's very light.

Serves 4

Calories per portion about 135

INGREDIENTS
2 eggs
215 g/7.7 oz carton evaporated semi-skimmed milk
25 ml/5 tsp instant coffee granules or powder
30 ml/2 tbsp granulated sweetener
10 ml/2 tsp powdered gelatine
60 ml/4 tbsp light crème fraîche
extra cocoa powder or ground cinnamon, to decorate

evaporated semi-skimmed milk

powdered gelatine

granulated sweetener

instant coffee

eggs

crème fraîche

cocoa powder

1 Separate one egg and reserve the white. Beat the yolk with the whole of the remaining egg.

2 Put the evaporated milk, coffee granules, sweetener and beaten eggs in a pan; whisk until evenly combined.

3 Put the pan over a low heat and stir constantly until the mixture is hot, but not boiling. Cook, stirring constantly, without boiling, until the mixture is slightly thickened and smooth.

4 Remove the pan from the heat. Sprinkle the gelatine over the pan and whisk until the gelatine has completely dissolved.

5 Spoon the coffee custard into four individual dishes or glasses and chill them until set.

6 Whisk the reserved egg white until stiff. Whisk in the crème fraîche and then spoon the mixture over the desserts. Sprinkle with cocoa or cinnamon and serve.

COOK'S TIP
It's important to ensure that the gelatine is completely dissolved before spooning the mixture into the dishes, otherwise the texture will not be smooth.

VARIATION
Greek yogurt can be used instead of the crème fraîche, if you prefer.

Mango and Ginger Clouds

The sweet, perfumed flavour of ripe mango combines beautifully with ginger, and this low-fat dessert makes the very most of them both.

Serves 6

Calories per portion about 125

INGREDIENTS
3 ripe mangoes
3 pieces stem ginger
45 ml/3 tbsp stem ginger syrup
75 g/3 oz/½ cup silken tofu
3 egg whites
6 pistachio nuts, chopped

tofu

mangoes

pistachio nuts

eggs

stem ginger in syrup

VARIATIONS
This dessert can be served lightly frozen. If you prefer not to use ginger, omit the ginger pieces and syrup and use 45 ml/3 tbsp clear honey instead.

1 Cut the mangoes in half, remove the stones and peel them. Roughly chop the flesh.

2 Put the mango flesh in a food processor bowl, with the ginger, syrup and tofu. Process until smooth. Spoon into a bowl.

3 Put the egg whites in a bowl and whisk them until they form soft peaks. Fold them lightly into the mango mixture.

4 Spoon the mixture into wide dishes or glasses and chill before serving, sprinkled with the chopped pistachios.

Gooseberry Cheese Cooler

Gooseberries are one of the less common summer fruits, so they're well worth snapping up when you can get them.

Serves 4

Calories per portion about 100

INGREDIENTS
500 g/1 lb/4 cups fresh or frozen
  gooseberries
1 small orange
15 ml/1 tbsp clear honey
250 g/9 oz/1 cup half-fat cottage
  cheese

orange

gooseberries

clear honey

cottage cheese

COOK'S TIP

If fresh or frozen gooseberries are not available, canned ones are often packed in heavy syrup, so it's best to substitute a different fresh fruit. Rhubarb or apples are also ideal for this recipe.

1 Top and tail the gooseberries and place them in a pan. Finely grate the rind from the orange and squeeze out the juice; then add them both to the pan. Cover the pan and cook gently, stirring occasionally, until the fruit is tender.

2 Remove from the heat and stir in the honey. Purée the gooseberries with their juice in a food processor until almost smooth. Cool.

3 Press the cottage cheese through a sieve, or process it in a food processor, until smooth. Stir half the cooled gooseberry purée into the cheese.

4 Spoon the cheese mixture into four serving dishes or glasses. Top each with a spoonful of the gooseberry purée. Serve chilled.

Passion-fruit and Apple Foam

Passion-fruit have an exotic, scented flavour that makes this simple apple dessert very special; if passion-fruit are not available, use two finely chopped kiwi fruit instead.

Serves 4

Calories per portion about 75

INGREDIENTS
500 g/1 lb cooking apples
90 ml/6 tbsp apple juice
3 passion-fruit
3 egg whites
1 red-skinned apple, to decorate
lemon juice

apple juice

lemon

cooking apples

red-skinned apple

eggs

passion-fruit

1 Peel, core and roughly chop the cooking apples and place them in a pan, with the apple juice.

2 Bring to the boil, and then reduce the heat and cover the pan. Cook gently, stirring occasionally, until the apple is very tender.

3 Remove from the heat and beat the apple mixture with a wooden spoon until it becomes a fairly smooth purée (or purée the apple in a food processor).

4 Cut the passion-fruit in half and scoop out the flesh. Stir the flesh into the apple purée.

5 Place the egg whites in a clean, dry bowl and whisk them until they form soft peaks. Fold the egg whites into the apple mixture. Spoon the apple foam into four serving dishes.

COOK'S TIP

It's important to use a good cooking apple, such as a Bramley, for this recipe, because the fluffy texture of a cooking apple breaks down easily to a purée. You can use dessert apples, but you will find it easier to purée them in a food processor.

6 Thinly slice the red-skinned apple and brush the slices with lemon juice, to prevent them from browning. Arrange the slices on top of the apple foam and serve cold.

Fluffy Banana and Pineapple Mousse

This light, low-fat mousse looks very impressive but is really very easy to make, especially with a food processor.

Serves 6

Calories per portion about 160

INGREDIENTS
2 ripe bananas
225 g/8 oz/1 cup cottage cheese
425 g/15 oz can pineapple chunks or pieces in juice
15 ml/1 tbsp/1 sachet powdered gelatine
2 egg whites

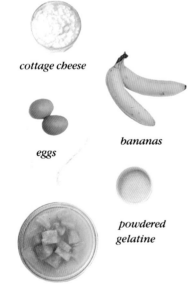

cottage cheese

eggs

bananas

powdered gelatine

pineapple chunks

COOK'S TIP

For a simpler way of serving, use a 1-litre/1¾-pint/4-cup serving dish, which will hold all the mixture, and do not tie a collar around the edge. Decorate the top with the reserved fruit as in the recipe.

1 Tie a double band of non-stick baking paper around a 600 ml/1-pint/2½-cup soufflé dish, to come 5 cm/2 in above the rim.

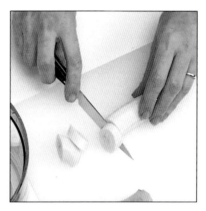

2 Peel and chop one banana and place it in a food processor with the cottage cheese. Process them until smooth.

3 Drain the pineapple, reserving the juice, and reserve a few pieces or chunks for decoration. Add the rest to the mixture in the processor and process for a few seconds until finely chopped.

4 Dissolve the gelatine in 60 ml/4 tbsp of the reserved pineapple juice. Stir the gelatine quickly into the fruit mixture.

5 Quickly whisk the egg whites until they hold soft peaks and fold them lightly and evenly into the mixture. Tip the mousse mixture into the prepared dish, smooth the surface and chill it in the refrigerator, until set.

6 When the mousse is set, carefully remove the paper collar. Decorate the mousse with the reserved banana and pineapple.

Frozen Apple and Blackberry Terrine

Apples and blackberries are a classic autumn combination; they really complement each other. This pretty, three-layered terrine can be frozen, so you can enjoy it at any time of year.

VARIATION

For a quicker version the mixture can be set without the layering. Purée the apples and blackberries together, stir the dissolved gelatine and whisked egg whites into the mixture, turn the whole thing into the tin and leave the mixture to set.

Serves 6

Calories per portion about 75

INGREDIENTS
500 g/1 lb cooking or eating apples
300 ml/½ pint/1¼ cups sweet cider
15 ml/1 tbsp clear honey
5 ml/1 tsp vanilla essence
200 g/7 oz/2 cups fresh or frozen and
   thawed blackberries
15 ml/1 tbsp/1 sachet powdered
   gelatine
2 egg whites
fresh apple slices and blackberries,
   to decorate

1 Peel, core and chop the apples and place them in a pan, with half the cider. Bring the cider to the boil, and then cover the pan and let the apples simmer gently until tender.

2 Tip the apples into a food processor and process them to a smooth purée. Stir in the honey and vanilla. Add half the blackberries to half the apple purée, and then process again until smooth. Sieve to remove the pips.

3 Heat the remaining cider until it's almost boiling, and then sprinkle the gelatine over and stir until the gelatine has completely dissolved. Add half the gelatine to the apple purée and half to the blackberry purée.

sweet cider

vanilla essence

clear honey

eggs

blackberries

powdered gelatine

4 Leave the purées to cool until almost set. Whisk the egg whites until they are stiff. Quickly fold them into the apple purée. Remove half the purée to another bowl. Stir the remaining whole blackberries into half the apple purée, and then tip this into a 1.75-litre/3-pint/7½-cup loaf tin, packing it down firmly.

5 Top with the blackberry purée and spread it evenly. Finally, add a layer of the apple purée and smooth it evenly. If necessary, freeze each layer until firm before adding the next.

6 Freeze until firm. To serve, allow to stand at room temperature for about 20 minutes to soften, and then serve in slices, decorated with fresh apples and blackberries.

Christmas Cranberry Bombe

This is a much lighter alternative to Christmas pudding, but still very festive and luxurious.

Serves 6

Calories per portion about 185

INGREDIENTS
FOR THE SORBET CENTRE
175 g/6 oz/2 cups fresh or frozen
   cranberries
150 ml/¼ pint/⅔ cup orange juice
finely grated rind of ½ orange
2.5 ml/½ tsp mixed spice
50 g/2 oz/4 tbsp golden caster sugar

FOR THE OUTER LAYER
1 quantity Buttermilk Vanilla Ice
   Cream (see page 61)
30 ml/2 tbsp chopped angelica
30 ml/2 tbsp mixed peel
15 ml/1 tbsp flaked almonds, toasted

candied peel

orange

cranberries

flaked almonds

angelica

1 Put the cranberries, orange juice, rind and spice in a pan and cook gently until the cranberries are soft. Add the sugar, then purée in a food processor until almost smooth, but still with some texture. Leave to cool.

2 Allow the vanilla ice to soften slightly then stir in the chopped angelica, mixed peel and almonds.

3 Pack into a 1.2-litre/2-pint/5-cup pudding basin and hollow out the centre. Freeze until firm.

4 Fill the hollowed-out centre of the bombe with cranberry mixture, smooth over and freeze until firm. To serve, allow to soften slightly at room temperature, turn out and serve in slices.

Buttermilk Vanilla Ice Cream

Enriched with just a little double cream, this unusual ice cream tastes far more luxurious than it really is. Serve it with fresh fruit or fruit purée.

Serves 4

Calories per portion about 150

INGREDIENTS
250 ml/8 fl oz/1 cup buttermilk
60 ml/4 tbsp double cream
1 vanilla pod or 2.5 ml/½ tsp vanilla
    essence
2 eggs
30 ml/2 tbsp clear honey

clear honey

eggs

buttermilk

double cream

vanilla pod

VARIATIONS

This basic vanilla ice cream can be used as a base for other flavours: stir in puréed or chopped fruit, dissolved instant coffee or citrus rind, or coat the frozen roll in a layer of desiccated coconut or chopped nuts.

1 Place the buttermilk and cream in a pan with the vanilla pod, if using, and heat gently over a low heat until the mixture is almost boiling. Remove the vanilla pod.

2 Place the eggs in a bowl over a pan of hot water and whisk until they are pale and thick. Pour in the heated buttermilk in a thin stream, whisking hard. Continue whisking over the hot water until the mixture thickens slightly.

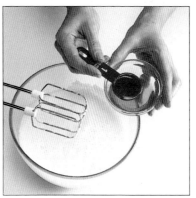

3 Whisk in the honey and vanilla essence, if using. Spoon the mixture into a freezer container and freeze until it's firm.

4 When the mixture is firm enough to hold its shape, spoon it on to a sheet of non-stick baking paper. Form it into a long sausage shape and roll it up in the paper. Freeze again until firm. Serve the ice cream in slices.

Summer Fruit Salad Ice Cream

What could be more cooling on a hot summer day than fresh summer fruits, lightly frozen in this irresistible ice?

COOK'S TIP
Red grape juice has a good flavour and improves the colour of the ice, but if it is not available, use cranberry, apple or orange juice instead.

Serves 6

Calories per portion about 130

INGREDIENTS
900 g/2 lb/4½ cups mixed soft
   summer fruit, such as raspberries,
   strawberries, blackcurrants,
   redcurrants, etc
2 eggs
225 g/8 oz/1 cup Greek yogurt
175 ml/6 fl oz/¾ cup red grape juice
15 ml/1 tbsp/1 sachet powdered
   gelatine

red grape juice

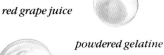

powdered gelatine

Greek yogurt

eggs

summer fruits

1 Reserve half the fruit and purée the rest in a food processor, or rub it through a sieve to make a smooth purée.

2 Separate the eggs and whisk the yolks and the yogurt into the fruit purée.

3 Heat the grape juice until it's almost boiling, and then remove it from the heat. Sprinkle the gelatine over the grape juice and stir to dissolve the gelatine completely.

4 Whisk the dissolved gelatine mixture into the fruit purée and then pour the mixture into a freezer container. Freeze until half-frozen and slushy in consistency.

5 Whisk the egg whites until they are stiff. Quickly fold them into the half-frozen mixture.

6 Return to the freezer and freeze until almost firm. Scoop into individual dishes or glasses and add the reserved soft fruits.

Mango and Lime Sorbet in Lime Shells

This richly flavoured sorbet looks pretty served in the lime shells, but is also good served in scoops for a more traditional presentation.

Serves 4

Calories per portion about 45

INGREDIENTS
4 large limes
1 medium-size ripe mango
7.5 ml/½ tbsp powdered gelatine
2 egg whites
15 ml/1 tbsp granulated sweetener
lime rind strips, to decorate

eggs

mango

granulated sweetener

limes

powdered gelatine

COOK'S TIP

If you have lime juice left over from this recipe, it will freeze well for future use. Pour it into a small freezer container, seal it and freeze for up to six months. Or freeze it in useful measured amounts; pour 15 ml/1 tbsp into each compartment of an ice-cube tray and freeze the tray.

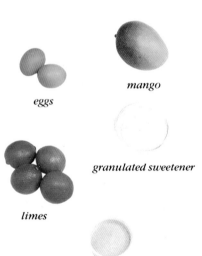

1 Cut a thick slice from the top of each of the limes, and then cut a thin slice from the bottom end so that the limes will stand upright. Squeeze out the juice from the limes. Use a small knife to remove all the membrane from the centre.

2 Halve, stone, peel and chop the mango and purée the flesh in a food processor with 30 ml/2 tbsp of the lime juice. Dissolve the gelatine in 45 ml/ 3 tbsp of lime juice and stir it into the mango mixture.

3 Whisk the egg whites until they hold soft peaks. Whisk in the sweetener. Fold the egg white mixture quickly into the mango mixture. Spoon the sorbet into the lime shells. Any leftover sorbet that will not fit into the lime shells can be frozen in small ramekins.

4 Place the filled shells in the freezer until the sorbet is firm. Overwrap the shells in clear film. Before serving, allow the shells to stand at room temperature for about 10 minutes; decorate them with strips of lime rind.

Rhubarb and Orange Water-ice

Pretty pink rhubarb, with sweet oranges and honey – the perfect sweet ice.

Serves 4

Calories per portion about 40

INGREDIENTS
350 g/12 oz pink rhubarb
1 medium-size orange
15 ml/1 tbsp clear honey
5 ml/1 tsp powdered gelatine
orange slices, to decorate

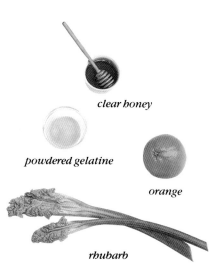

clear honey

powdered gelatine

orange

rhubarb

1 Trim the rhubarb and slice into 2.5 cm/1 in lengths. Place the rhubarb in a pan.

2 Finely grate the rind from the orange and squeeze out the juice. Add about half the orange juice and the grated rind to the rhubarb in the pan and allow to simmer until the rhubarb is just tender. Stir in the honey.

COOK'S TIP
Most pink, forced rhubarb is naturally quite sweet, but if yours is not, you can add a little more honey, sugar or artificial sweetener to taste.

3 Heat the remaining orange juice and stir in the gelatine to dissolve. Stir it into the rhubarb. Tip the whole mixture into a rigid freezer container and freeze it until it's slushy, about 2 hours.

4 Remove the mixture from the freezer and beat it well to break up the ice crystals. Return the water-ice to the freezer and freeze it again until firm. Allow the water-ice to soften slightly at room temperature before serving.

Cinnamon and Apricot Soufflés

Don't expect this to be difficult simply because it's a soufflé – it really couldn't be easier, and, best of all, it's very low in calories.

Serves 4

Calories per portion about 95

INGREDIENTS
3 eggs
115 g/4 oz/½ cup apricot fruit spread
finely grated rind of ½ lemon
5 ml/1 tsp ground cinnamon
extra cinnamon, to decorate

eggs

apricot fruit spread

lemon rind

ground cinnamon

1 Preheat the oven to 190°C/375°F/ Gas 5. Lightly grease four individual soufflé dishes and dust them lightly with flour.

2 Separate the eggs and place the yolks in a bowl with the fruit spread, lemon rind and cinnamon.

3 Whisk hard until the mixture is thick and pale in colour.

4 Place the egg whites in a clean bowl and whisk them until they are stiff enough to hold soft peaks.

5 Using a metal spoon or spatula, fold the egg whites evenly into the yolk mixture.

COOK'S TIP

Puréed fresh or well drained canned fruit can be used instead of the apricot spread, but make sure the mixture is not too wet, or the soufflé will not rise properly.

6 Divide the soufflé mixture between the prepared dishes and bake for 10–15 minutes, until well-risen and golden brown. Serve immediately, dusted with a little extra ground cinnamon.

Orange Yogurt Brûlées

A luxurious treat, but one that is much lower in fat than the classic brûlées, which are made with cream, eggs and large amounts of sugar.

Serves 4

Calories per portion about 185

INGREDIENTS
2 medium-size oranges
150 g/5 oz/⅔ cup Greek yogurt
50 g/2 oz/¼ cup crème fraîche
45 ml/3 tbsp golden caster sugar
30 ml/2 tbsp light muscovado sugar

golden caster sugar

light muscovado sugar

crème fraîche

oranges

Greek yogurt

COOK'S TIP

For a lighter version, simply use 200 g/7 oz/⅞ cup low-fat natural yogurt instead of the Greek yogurt and crème fraîche.

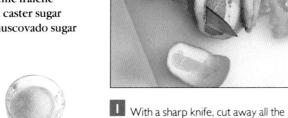

1 With a sharp knife, cut away all the peel and white pith from the oranges and chop the fruit. Or, if there's time, segment the oranges, removing all the membrane.

2 Place the fruit in the bottom of four individual flameproof dishes. Mix together the yogurt and crème fraîche and spoon the mixture over the oranges.

3 Mix together the two sugars and sprinkle them evenly over the tops of the dishes.

4 Place the dishes under a preheated, very hot grill for 3–4 minutes or until the sugar melts and turns to a rich golden brown. Serve warm or cold.

Figs with Ricotta Cream

Fresh, ripe figs are full of natural sweetness, and need little adornment. This simple recipe makes the most of their beautiful, intense flavour.

Serves 4

Calories per portion about 110

INGREDIENTS
4 ripe, fresh figs
115 g/4 oz/½ cup ricotta or cottage
   cheese
45 ml/3 tbsp crème fraîche
15 ml/1 tbsp clear honey
2.5 ml/½ tsp vanilla essence
freshly grated nutmeg, to decorate

vanilla essence

clear honey

crème fraîche

ricotta cheese

figs

nutmeg

1 Trim the stalks from the figs. Make four cuts through each fig from the stalk-end, cutting them almost through but leaving them joined at the base.

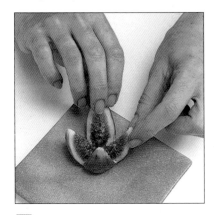

2 Place the figs on serving plates and open them out.

COOK'S TIP
If you prefer, the honey can be omitted and replaced with a little artificial sweetener.

3 Mix together the ricotta or cottage cheese, crème fraîche, honey and vanilla.

4 Spoon a little ricotta cream on to each plate and sprinkle with grated nutmeg to serve.

Quick Apricot Blender Whip

One of the quickest desserts you could make – and also one of the prettiest.

Serves 4

Calories per portion about 125

INGREDIENTS
400 g/14 oz can apricot halves in juice
15 ml/1 tbsp Grand Marnier or brandy
175 g/6 oz/¾ cup Greek yogurt
30 ml/2 tbsp flaked almonds

Greek yogurt

Grand Marnier

apricot halves

flaked almonds

1 Drain the juice from the apricots and place the fruit and liqueur in a blender or food processor.

2 Process the apricots until smooth.

3 Spoon the fruit purée and yogurt in alternate spoonfuls into four tall glasses or glass dishes, swirling them together slightly to give a marbled effect.

4 Lightly toast the almonds until they are golden. Let them cool slightly and then sprinkle them on top.

COOK'S TIP

For an even lighter dessert, use low-fat instead of Greek yogurt, and, if you prefer to omit the liqueur, add a little of the fruit juice from the can.

Pineapple Wedges with Allspice and Lime

Fresh pineapple is easy to prepare and always looks very festive, so this dish is perfect for easy entertaining.

Serves 4

Calories per portion about 65

INGREDIENTS
1 medium-size, ripe pineapple
1 lime
15 ml/1 tbsp dark muscovado sugar
5 ml/1 tsp ground allspice

ground allspice   *pineapple*

muscovado sugar

lime

VARIATION

For a quick hot dish, place the pineapple slices on a baking sheet, sprinkle them with the lime juice, sugar and allspice and place them under a hot grill for 3–4 minutes, or until golden and bubbling. Sprinkle with shreds of lime zest and serve.

1 Cut the pineapple lengthways into quarters and remove the core.

2 Loosen the flesh, by sliding a knife between the flesh and the skin. Cut the flesh into slices, leaving it on the skin.

3 Remove a few shreds of rind from the lime and then squeeze out the juice.

4 Sprinkle the pineapple with the lime juice and rind, sugar and allspice. Serve immediately, or chill for up to an hour.

Raspberry Muesli Layer

As well as being a delicious, low-fat, high-fibre dessert, this can also be served for a quick, healthy breakfast.

Serves 4

Calories per portion about 115

INGREDIENTS
225 g/8 oz/2¼ cups fresh or frozen
  and thawed raspberries
225 g/8 oz/1 cup low-fat natural
  yogurt
75 g/3 oz/½ cup Swiss-style muesli

raspberries

Swiss-style muesli

natural yogurt

1 Reserve four raspberries for decoration, and then spoon a few raspberries into four stemmed glasses or glass dishes.

2 Top the raspberries with a spoonful of yogurt in each glass.

3 Sprinkle a layer of muesli over the yogurt.

4 Repeat with the raspberries and other ingredients. Top each with a whole raspberry.

COOK'S TIP

This recipe can be made in advance and stored in the fridge for several hours, or overnight if you're serving it for breakfast.

Brazilian Coffee Bananas

Rich, lavish and sinful-looking, this dessert takes only about 2 minutes to make!

Serves 4

Calories per portion about 195

INGREDIENTS
4 small ripe bananas
15 ml/1 tbsp instant coffee granules or
   powder
15 ml/1 tbsp hot water
30 ml/2 tbsp dark muscovado sugar
250 g/9 oz/1⅛ cups Greek yogurt
15 ml/1 tbsp toasted flaked almonds

bananas

Greek yogurt

flaked almonds

instant coffee

dark muscovado sugar

1 Peel and slice one banana and mash the remaining three with a fork.

2 Dissolve the coffee in the hot water and stir into the mashed bananas.

3 Spoon a little of the mashed banana mixture into four serving dishes and sprinkle with sugar. Top with a spoonful of yogurt, then repeat until all the ingredients are used up.

4 Swirl the last layer of yogurt for a marbled effect. Finish with a few banana slices and flaked almonds. Serve cold. Best eaten within about an hour of making.

VARIATION

For a special occasion, add a dash – just a dash – of dark rum or brandy to the bananas for extra richness. 15 ml/1 tbsp of rum or brandy adds about 30 calories.

Prune and Orange Pots

A simple, storecupboard dessert, made in minutes.
It can be served straight away, but it's best chilled
for about half an hour before serving.

Serves 4

Calories per portion about 110

INGREDIENTS
225 g/8 oz/1½ cups ready-to-eat dried
   prunes
150 ml/¼ pint/⅔ cup orange juice
225 g/8 oz/1 cup low-fat natural
   yogurt
shreds of orange rind, to decorate

orange juice

natural yogurt

orange rind

prunes

VARIATION

This dessert can also be made with
other ready-to-eat dried fruit, such as
apricots or peaches. For a special
occasion, add a dash of brandy or
Cointreau with the yogurt.

1 Remove the stones from the prunes
and roughly chop them. Place them in a
pan with the orange juice.

2 Bring the juice to the boil, stirring.
Reduce the heat, cover and leave to
simmer for 5 minutes, until the prunes are
tender and the liquid is reduced by half.

3 Remove from the heat, allow to cool
slightly and then beat well with a wooden
spoon, until the fruit breaks down to a
rough purée.

4 Transfer mixture to a bowl. Stir in
the yogurt, swirling the yogurt and fruit
purée together lightly, to give an
attractive marbled effect.

5 Spoon the mixture into stemmed
glasses or individual dishes, smoothing
the tops.

6 Top each pot with a few shreds
of orange rind, to decorate. Chill
before serving.

Minted Raspberry Bavarois

A sophisticated dessert that can be made a day in advance for a special dinner party.

Serves 6

Calories per portion about 145

INGREDIENTS
450 g/1 lb/5½ cups fresh or frozen
    and thawed raspberries
30 ml/2 tbsp icing sugar
30 ml/2 tbsp lemon juice
15 ml/1 tbsp finely chopped fresh mint
30 ml/2 tbsp/2 sachets powdered
    gelatine
75 ml/5 tbsp boiling water
300 ml/½ pint/1¼ cups custard,
    made with skimmed milk
250 g/9 oz/1⅛ cups Greek yogurt
fresh mint sprigs, to decorate

skimmed-milk custard

icing sugar

Greek yogurt

powdered gelatine

lemon

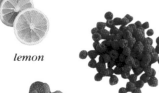

mint   *raspberries*

COOK'S TIP
You can make this dessert using frozen raspberries, which have a good colour and flavour. Allow them to thaw at room temperature, and use any juice in the jelly.

1 Reserve a few raspberries for decoration. Place the raspberries, icing sugar and lemon juice in a food processor and process them until smooth.

2 Press the purée through a sieve to remove the raspberry pips. Add the mint. You should have about 500 ml/1 pint/2½ cups of purée.

3 Sprinkle 5 ml/1 tsp of the gelatine over 30 ml/2 tbsp of the boiling water and stir until the gelatine has dissolved. Stir into 150 ml/¼ pint/⅔ cup of the fruit purée.

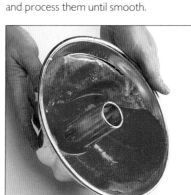

4 Pour this jelly into a 1-litre/1¾-pint/4-cup mould, and leave the mould to chill in the refrigerator until the jelly is just on the point of setting. Tip the tin to swirl the setting jelly around the sides, and then leave to chill until the jelly has set completely.

5 Stir the remaining fruit purée into the custard and yogurt. Dissolve the rest of the gelatine in the remaining water and stir it in quickly.

6 Pour the raspberry custard into the mould and leave it to chill until it has set completely. To serve, dip the mould quickly into hot water and then turn it out and decorate it with the reserved raspberries and the mint sprigs.

Papaya Skewers with Passion-fruit Coulis

Tropical fruits, full of natural sweetness, make a simple, exotic dessert.

Serves 6

Calories per portion about 75

INGREDIENTS
3 ripe papayas
10 passion-fruit or kiwi fruit
30 ml/2 tbsp lime juice
30 ml/2 tbsp icing sugar
30 ml/2 tbsp white rum
toasted coconut, to garnish (optional)

icing sugar

papayas

passion fruit

lime

COOK'S TIP

If you are short of time, the passion-fruit flesh can be used as it is, without puréeing or sieving. Simply scoop the flesh from the skins and mix it with the lime, sugar and rum. Kiwi fruit will still need to be puréed, however.

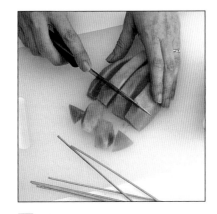

1 Cut the papayas in half and scoop out the seeds. Peel them and cut the flesh into even-size chunks. Thread the chunks on to six bamboo skewers.

2 Halve eight of the passion-fruit or kiwi fruit and scoop out the flesh. Purée the flesh for a few seconds in a blender or food processor.

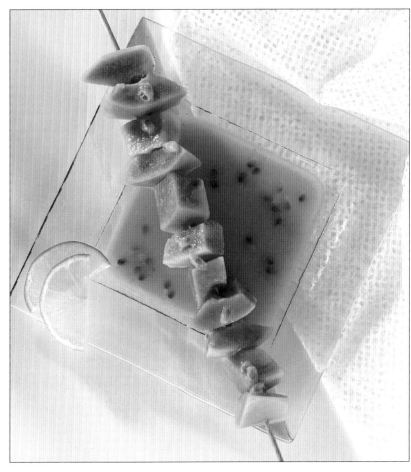

3 Press the pulp through a sieve and discard the seeds. Add the lime juice, icing sugar and rum, and then stir well until the sugar has dissolved.

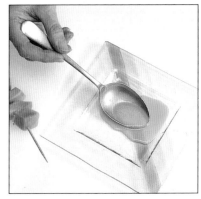

4 Spoon a little coulis on to six serving plates. Place the skewers on top. Scoop the flesh from the remaining passion-fruit or kiwi fruit and spoon it over. Sprinkle with a little toasted coconut, if you like, and serve.

Cool Green Fruit Salad

A sophisticated, simple fruit salad for any time of year.

Serves 6

Calories per portion about 100

INGREDIENTS
3 Ogen or Galia melons
115 g/4 oz green seedless grapes
2 kiwi fruit
1 star-fruit
1 green-skinned apple
1 lime
175 ml/6 fl oz/¾ cup sparkling
   grape juice

sparkling grape juice

melons

seedless grapes

kiwi fruit

star-fruit

lime

green-skinned apple

COOK'S TIP

If you're serving this dessert on a hot summer day, serve the filled melon shells nestling on a platter of crushed ice to keep them beautifully cool.

1 Cut the melons in half and scoop out the seeds. Keeping the shells intact, scoop out the flesh with a melon baller, or scoop it out with a spoon and cut into bite-size cubes. Reserve the melon shells.

2 Remove any stems from the grapes, and, if they are large, cut them in half. Peel and chop the kiwi fruit. Thinly slice the star-fruit. Core and thinly slice the apple and place the slices in a bowl, with the melon, grapes, kiwi fruit and star-fruit.

3 Thinly pare the rind from the lime and cut it in fine strips. Blanch the strips in boiling water for 30 seconds, and then drain them and rinse them in cold water. Squeeze the juice from the lime and toss it into the fruit.

4 Spoon the prepared fruit into the reserved melon shells and chill the shells in the refrigerator until required. Just before serving, spoon the sparkling grape juice over the fruit and scatter it with the lime rind.

Apricot and Orange Roulade

This elegant dessert is very good served with a spoonful of Greek yogurt or crème fraîche.

Serves 6

Calories per portion about 170

INGREDIENTS
FOR THE ROULADE
4 egg whites
115 g/4 oz/⅔ cup golden caster sugar
50 g/2 oz/¾ cup plain flour
finely grated rind of 1 small orange
45 ml/3 tbsp orange juice

FOR THE FILLING
115 g/4 oz/½ cup ready-to-eat dried
 apricots
150 ml/¼ pint/⅔ cup orange juice

TO DECORATE
10 ml/2 tsp icing sugar, to sprinkle
shreds of orange zest, to decorate

orange

orange juice

eggs

golden caster sugar

plain flour

dried apricots

COOK'S TIP
Make and bake the sponge mixture a day in advance and keep it, rolled with the paper, in a cool place. Fill it with the fruit purée 2–3 hours before serving. The sponge can also be frozen for up to 2 months; thaw it at room temperature and fill it as above.

1 Preheat the oven to 200°C/400°F/ Gas 6. Grease a 23 × 33 cm/9 × 13 in Swiss-roll tin and line it with non-stick baking paper. Grease the paper.

2 To make the roulade, place the egg whites in a large bowl and whisk them until they hold soft peaks. Gradually add the sugar, whisking hard between each addition.

3 Fold in the flour, orange rind and juice. Spoon the mixture into the prepared tin and spread it evenly.

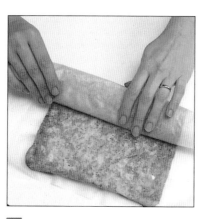

4 Bake for 15–18 minutes, or until the sponge is firm and light golden in colour. Turn out on to a sheet of non-stick baking paper and roll it up loosely from one short side. Leave to cool.

5 Roughly chop the apricots and place them in a pan, with the orange juice. Cover the pan and leave to simmer until most of the liquid has been absorbed. Purée the apricots in a food processor.

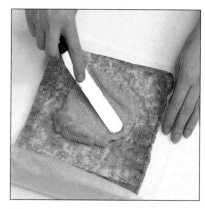

6 Unroll the roulade and spread with the apricot mixture. Roll up, arrange strips of paper diagonally across the roll, sprinkle lightly with lines of icing sugar, remove the paper and scatter with orange zest to serve.

Foamy Yogurt Ring with Tropical Fruit

An impressive, light and colourful dessert with a truly tropical flavour.

Serves 6

Calories per portion about 90

INGREDIENTS
FOR THE YOGURT RING
175 ml/6 fl oz/¾ cup tropical fruit juice
15 ml/1 tbsp/1 sachet powdered gelatine
3 egg whites
150 g/5 oz/⅔ cup low-fat natural yogurt
finely grated rind of 1 lime

FOR THE FILLING
1 mango
2 kiwi fruit
10–12 cape gooseberries
juice of 1 lime

mango

natural yogurt

tropical fruit juice

eggs

kiwi fruit

lime

powdered gelatine

cape gooseberries

1 Place the tropical fruit juice in a small pan and sprinkle the gelatine over. Heat gently until the gelatine has dissolved.

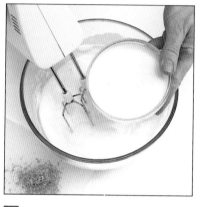

2 Whisk the egg whites in a clean, dry bowl until they hold soft peaks. Continue whisking hard, whilst gradually adding the yogurt and lime rind.

3 Continue whisking hard and pour in the hot gelatine mixture in a steady stream, until everything is evenly mixed.

4 Quickly pour the mixture into a 1.5-litre/2½-pint/6¼-cup ring mould. Chill the mould in the refrigerator until set. The mixture will separate into two layers.

5 Halve, stone, peel and dice the mango. Peel and slice the kiwi fruit. Remove the outer leaves from the cape gooseberries and cut in half. Toss all the fruits together and stir in the lime juice.

VARIATION

Any mixture of fruit works in this recipe, depending on the season. Try using apple juice in the ring mixture and fill it with luscious, red summer fruits.

6 Run a knife around the edge of the ring to loosen the mixture. Dip the tin quickly into cold water and then turn it out on to a serving plate. Spoon all the prepared fruit into the centre of the ring and serve immediately.

Latticed Peaches

An elegant dessert; it certainly doesn't look low in fat, but it really is. Use canned peach halves when fresh peaches are out of season, or if you're short of time.

Serves 6

Calories per portion about 170

INGREDIENTS
FOR THE PASTRY
115 g/4 oz/1 cup plain flour
45 ml/3 tbsp butter or sunflower
  margarine
45 ml/3 tbsp low-fat natural yogurt
30 ml/2 tbsp orange juice
skimmed milk

FOR THE FILLING
3 ripe peaches or nectarines
45 ml/3 tbsp ground almonds
30 ml/2 tbsp low-fat natural yogurt
finely grated rind of 1 small orange
1.25 ml/¼ tsp natural almond essence

FOR THE SAUCE
1 ripe peach or nectarine
45 ml/3 tbsp orange juice

orange

plain flour

peaches

almond essence

ground almonds

COOK'S TIP

This dessert is best eaten fairly fresh from the oven, as the pastry can toughen slightly if left to stand. So assemble the peaches in their pastry on a baking sheet, chill in the refrigerator, and bake just before serving.

1 For the pastry, sift the flour into a bowl and, using your fingertips, rub in the butter or margarine evenly. Stir in the yogurt and orange juice to bind the mixture to a firm dough.

2 Roll out about half the pastry thinly and use a biscuit cutter to stamp out rounds about 7.5 cm/3 in in diameter, slightly larger than the circumference of the peaches. Place on a lightly greased baking sheet.

3 Skin the peaches, halve and remove the stones. Mix together the almonds, yogurt, orange rind and almond essence. Spoon into the hollows of each peach half and place, cut side down, on to the pastry rounds.

4 Roll out the remaining pastry thinly and cut into thin strips. Arrange the strips over the peaches to form a lattice, brushing with milk to secure firmly. Trim off the ends neatly.

5 Chill in the refrigerator for 30 minutes. Preheat the oven to 200°C/400°F/Gas 6. Brush with milk and bake for 15–18 minutes, until golden brown.

6 For the sauce, skin the peach or nectarine and halve it to remove the stone. Place the flesh in a food processor, with the orange juice, and purée it until smooth. Serve the peaches hot, with the peach sauce spooned around.

Lemon Hearts with Strawberry Sauce

These elegant little hearts are light as air, and they are best made the day before your dinner party – which saves on last-minute panics as well!

Serves 6

Calories per portion about 140

INGREDIENTS
FOR THE HEARTS
175 g/6 oz/¾ cup ricotta cheese
150 ml/¼ pint/⅔ cup crème fraîche
   or soured cream
15 ml/1 tbsp granulated sweetener
finely grated rind of ½ lemon
30 ml/2 tbsp lemon juice
10 ml/2 tsp powdered gelatine
2 egg whites

FOR THE SAUCE
225 g/8 oz/2 cups fresh or frozen and
   thawed strawberries
15 ml/1 tbsp lemon juice

ricotta cheese

lemon

eggs

crème fraîche

powdered gelatine

strawberries

granulated sweetener

1 Beat the ricotta cheese until smooth. Stir in the crème fraîche, sweetener and lemon rind.

2 Place the lemon juice in a small bowl and sprinkle the gelatine over it. Place the bowl over a pan of hot water and stir to dissolve the gelatine completely.

3 Quickly stir the gelatine into the cheese mixture, mixing it in evenly.

4 Beat the egg whites until they form soft peaks. Quickly fold them into the cheese mixture.

5 Spoon the mixture into six lightly oiled, individual heart-shaped moulds and chill the moulds until set.

VARIATION

These little heart-shaped desserts are
the perfect choice for a romantic
dinner, but they don't have to be
heart-shaped – try setting the mixture
in individual fluted moulds, or even in
ordinary teacups.

6 Place the strawberries and lemon juice
in a blender and process until smooth.
Pour the sauce on to serving plates and
place the turned-out hearts on top.
Decorate with slices of strawberry.

Strawberry Rose-petal Pashka

This lighter version of a traditional Russian dessert is ideal for dinner parties – make it a day or two in advance for best results.

Serves 4

Calories per portion about 150

INGREDIENTS
350 g/12 oz/1½ cups cottage cheese
175 g/6 oz/¾ cup low-fat natural
  yogurt
30 ml/2 tbsp clear honey
2.5 ml/½ tsp rose-water
275 g/10 oz/2½ cups strawberries
handful of scented pink rose petals, to
  decorate

clear honey

cottage cheese

rose-water

strawberries

natural yogurt

COOK'S TIP
The flowerpot shape is traditional for pashka, but you could make it in any shape – the small porcelain heart-shaped moulds with draining holes usually used for *coeurs à la crème* make a pretty alternative.

1 Drain any free liquid from the cottage cheese and tip the cheese into a sieve. Use a wooden spoon to rub it through the sieve into a bowl.

2 Stir the yogurt, honey and rose-water into the cheese.

3 Roughly chop about half the strawberries and stir them into the cheese mixture.

4 Line a new, clean flowerpot or a sieve with fine muslin and tip the cheese mixture in. Leave it to drain over a bowl for several hours, or overnight.

5 Invert the flowerpot or sieve on to a serving plate, turn out the pashka and remove the muslin.

6 Decorate with the reserved strawberries and rose petals. Serve chilled.

Mandarins in Orange-flower Syrup

Mandarins, tangerines, clementines, mineolas: any of these lovely citrus fruits are suitable for this recipe.

Serves 4

Calories per portion about 85

INGREDIENTS
10 mandarins
15 ml/1 tbsp icing sugar
10 ml/2 tsp orange-flower water
15 ml/1 tbsp chopped pistachio nuts

orange-flower water

pistachio nuts

mandarins

icing sugar

COOK'S TIP

The mandarins look very attractive if you leave them whole, especially if there is a large quantity for a special occasion, but you may prefer to separate the segments.

1 Thinly pare a little of the coloured zest from one mandarin and cut it into fine shreds for decoration. Squeeze the juice from two mandarins and reserve it.

2 Peel the remaining fruit, removing as much of the white pith as possible. Arrange the whole fruit in a wide dish.

3 Mix the reserved juice, sugar and orange-flower water and pour it over the fruit. Cover the dish and chill for at least an hour.

4 Blanch the shreds of zest in boiling water for 30 seconds. Drain, leave to cool and sprinkle them over the mandarins, with the pistachio nuts, to serve.

Redcurrant Filo Baskets

Filo pastry is light as air and makes a very elegant dessert. It's also low in fat and it needs only a fine brushing of oil before use: a light oil such as sunflower is the best choice for this recipe.

Serves 6

Calories per portion about 130

INGREDIENTS
3 sheets filo pastry (about
    85 g/3½ oz)
15 ml/1 tbsp sunflower oil
175 g/6 oz/1½ cups redcurrants
200 g/7 oz/1 cup Greek yogurt
5 ml/1 tsp icing sugar

filo pastry

Greek yogurt

redcurrants

sunflower oil

icing sugar

1 Preheat the oven to 200°C/400°F/ Gas 6. Cut the sheets of filo pastry into 18 squares with sides about 10 cm/4 in long.

2 Brush each filo square very thinly with oil, and then arrange the squares overlapping in six small patty tins, layering them in threes. Bake for 6–8 minutes, until crisp and golden. Lift the baskets out carefully and leave them to cool on a wire rack.

3 Reserve a few sprigs of redcurrants on their stems for decoration and string the rest. Stir the currants into the yogurt.

4 Spoon the yogurt into the filo baskets. Decorate them with the reserved sprigs of redcurrants and sprinkle them with icing sugar to serve.

VARIATION
Strawberries or raspberries can be substituted for redcurrants, if they are not available.

Poached Pears in Maple-yogurt Sauce

An elegant dessert that is easier to make than it looks – poach the pears in advance, and have the cooled syrup ready to spoon on to the plates just before you serve.

Serves 6

Calories per portion about 140

INGREDIENTS
6 firm dessert pears
15 ml/1 tbsp lemon juice
250 ml/8 fl oz/1 cup sweet white wine
    or cider
thinly pared rind of 1 lemon
1 cinnamon stick
30 ml/2 tbsp maple syrup
2.5 ml/½ tsp arrowroot
150 g/5 oz/⅔ cup Greek yogurt

sweet white wine

Greek yogurt

pears

maple syrup

lemon

arrowroot

cinnamon stick

1 Thinly peel the pears, leaving them whole and with stalks. Brush them with lemon juice, to prevent them from browning. Use a potato peeler or small knife to scoop out the core from the base of each pear.

2 Place the pears in a wide, heavy pan and pour over the wine, with enough cold water almost to cover the pears.

3 Add the lemon rind and cinnamon stick, and then bring to the boil. Reduce the heat, cover the pan and simmer the pears gently for 30–40 minutes, or until tender. Turn the pears occasionally so that they cook evenly. Lift out the pears carefully, draining them well.

4 Bring the liquid to the boil and boil uncovered to reduce to about 100 ml/ 4 fl oz/½ cup. Strain and add the maple syrup. Blend a little of the liquid with the arrowroot. Return to the pan and cook, stirring, until thick and clear. Cool.

5 Slice each pear about three-quarters of the way through, leaving the slices attached at the stem end. Fan each pear out on a serving plate.

6 Stir 30 ml/2 tbsp of the cooled syrup into the yogurt and spoon it around the pears. Drizzle with the remaining syrup and serve immediately.

Blueberry and Orange Crêpe Baskets

Impress your guests with these pretty, fruit-filled crêpes. When blueberries are out of season, replace them with other soft fruit, such as raspberries.

Serves 6

Calories per portion about 160

INGREDIENTS
FOR THE PANCAKES
150 g/5 oz/1¼ cups plain flour
pinch salt
2 egg whites
200 ml/7 fl oz/⅞ cup skimmed milk
150 ml/¼ pint/⅔ cup orange juice

FOR THE FILLING
4 medium-size oranges
225 g/8 oz/2 cups blueberries

orange juice

oranges

eggs

blueberries

skimmed milk

1 Preheat the oven to 200°C/400°F/Gas 6. To make the pancakes, sift the flour and salt into a bowl. Make a well in the centre of the flour and add the egg whites, milk and orange juice. Whisk hard, until all the liquid has been incorporated and the batter is smooth and bubbly.

2 Lightly grease a heavy or non-stick pancake pan and heat it until it is very hot. Pour in just enough batter to cover the base of the pan, swirling it to cover the pan evenly.

3 Cook until the pancake has set and is golden, and then turn it to cook the other side. Remove the pancake to a sheet of absorbent kitchen paper, and then cook the remaining batter, to make 6–8 pancakes.

4 Place six small ovenproof bowls or moulds on a baking sheet and arrange the pancakes over these. Bake them in the oven for about 10 minutes, until they are crisp and set into shape. Carefully lift the 'baskets' off the moulds.

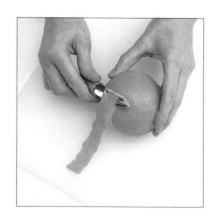

5 Pare a thin piece of orange rind from one orange and cut it in fine strips. Blanch the strips in boiling water for 30 seconds, rinse them in cold water and set them aside. Cut all the peel and white pith from all the oranges.

6 Divide the oranges into segments, catching the juice, combine with the blueberries and warm them gently. Spoon the fruit into the baskets and scatter the shreds of rind over the top. Serve with yogurt or light crème fraîche.

INDEX